3 AM POETRY

DEALING WITH UPS AND DOWNS OF LIFE

DRISH KING

Made with ♥ on the Notion Press Platform
www.notionpress.com

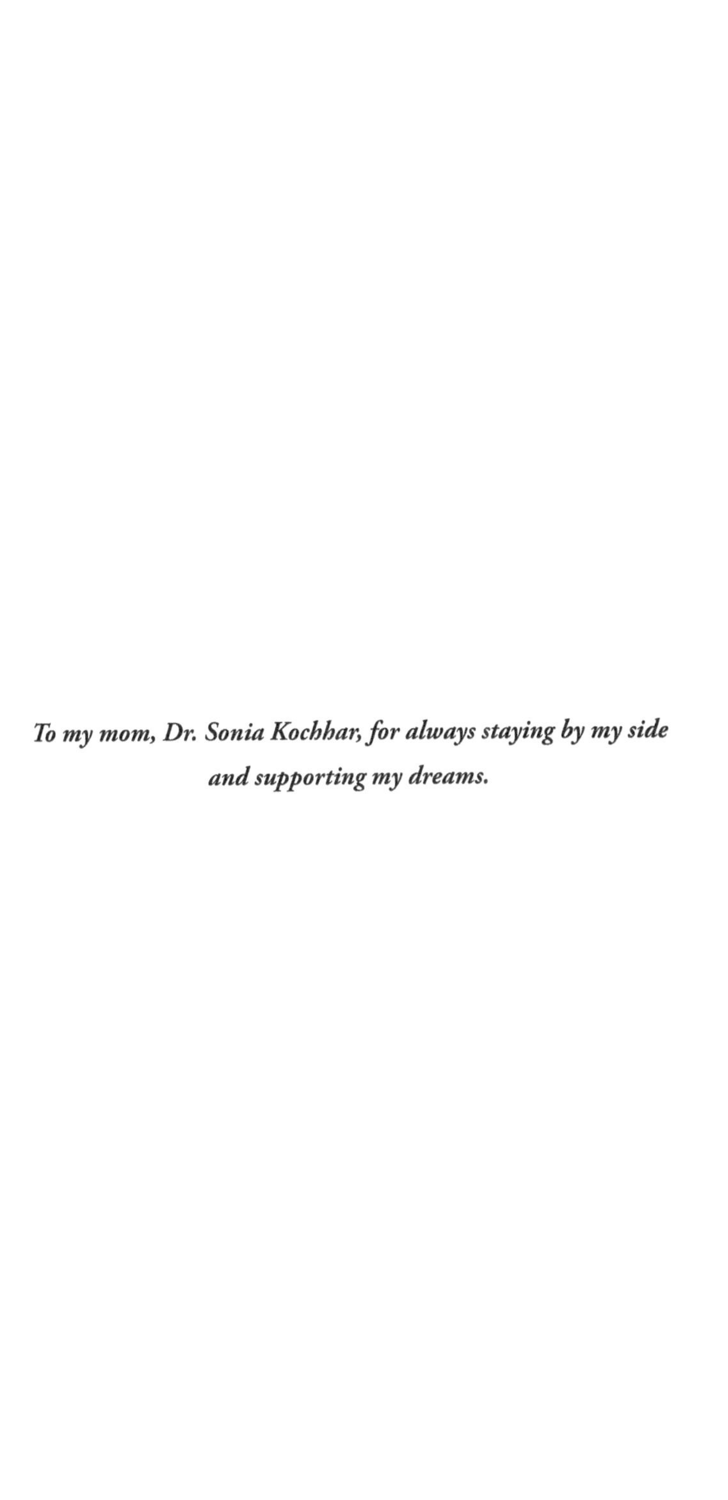

To my mom, Dr. Sonia Kochhar, for always staying by my side and supporting my dreams.

Contents

Contents

Contents

Preface

Poetry is the outcome of strong emotions, buried feelings, innovative ideas, and unpopular opinions. When my voice fails to support me, I turn to ink and pages. Playing with words and burying my emotions beneath them started as a hobby. But, it has now grown into a burning passion that is slowly consuming my mind and heart.

Writing books is addicting because it is a world you can control. However, writing poems is an even more dangerous addiction for at a point, it gets as necessary as breathing. You feel your soul melt into paper as all the overwhelming emotions flow out of your heart and settle on the paper, in the form of words and rhymes.

Paper has more patience than people. Poetry helps me to get all kinds of things off my chest and acts as a safe place for all my ideas and feelings. It's like my journal but one that is more cryptic and captures emotions rather than scenarios.

I have been writing poems for over four years now. I have become absolutely addicted to trapping all my feelings on a piece of paper. My previous poetry collection - Midnight Poetry: Dark Poems With Concealed Motivation, consisted of my top works which were my personal favorites.

However, the more I write poems, the more I improve at poetry and the longer my list of personal favorites gets. So, here I am publishing my brand new collection of poems - 3 AM Poetry: Dealing With Ups And Downs Of Life, the one you are holding in your hands right now.

Whether it be the rough pages you feel between your fingers or the hard body of your electronic device held tight in your hands, I promise you will feel waves of emotions crashing down on you as you continue reading this poem collection of another fifty handpicked poems I have written while dealing with the ups and downs of life myself.

> **"Life is really fair at being unfair.**
>
> *-Drish King (Author)* **"**

Whether it be the most jolly and positive person you have ever met or the friend who is always putting out fires and dodging one crisis after another, both of them have been through hell. The difference is that the former has walked through hell with a smile while the latter has crawled his way through hell while cursing his rotten luck.

All in all, it all comes down to *your* attitude. The way you tackle problems and whether you bounce back when life smacks you down or not is what makes the difference. A beggar might be happy and a billionaire might be getting crushed under responsibilities and stress.

These poems guide you and teach you how to deal with the ups and downs of life.

The poems have been divided into three segments - Breaking Down, Getting Up, and Short Odes, with three sweet bonus poems at the end as a reward for sticking with me and to serve as true motivation and potray care to help you struggle with your life's evils.

While the first two divisions are self-explanatory, the third one 'Short Odes' consists of several short poems for you to enjoy whether daily or in a single sitting, the choice is yours.

So, without wasting any more of your precious time, let's jump right into an endless sea of depressive ideas with a seabed of motivation, inspiring you to jump up, get above those waves, and remember what it actually feels like to breathe freely again.

Whether it be the ups or downs of life, or somewhere in between, these fifty poems have got your back in portraying every emotion.

So, what are you waiting for?

Dive right in...

Breaking Down

To the times you died inside to make yourself stronger...

To the times you cried alone to smile for the world...

To the times you wanted to scream at the top of your lungs but
remained quiet...

To the times you felt suffocated in your own mind...

To the times someone tore you apart and you didn't dish the
same...

To the times you fought yourself for someone who didn't deserve
all the care...

And lastly, to the times you gathered yourself when no one else
stepped forward to help...

***YOU right there, have walked through hell with a smile like you
own that goddamn place.***

1. I Am The One Responsible

============

It's not your fault I am what you don't need
It's my fault that you stabbed and I let it bleed
I am here because of my own deed
I myself planted my doom's seed

~

I am the one responsible
For everything happening to me
Was weak, couldn't pass the obstacle
My fault, more strong, I couldn't be

~

Now, I am here pleading life to set me free

~

Why can't I be like them?
'Cause you are unique', They say
Why do myself I condemn?
Can't I love myself in their way?

~

It's me, the problem ruining all good things
It's me, the monster, bad luck who brings

It's me, the chosen fairy, who failed to sprout wings

~

I am the one responsible
For everything happening to me
I dreamt the impossible
Wanted to be the one I could never be

~

Now, I am here pleading life to set me free

~

I did all those things I shouldn't have done
You pointed out the flaws already there
I was the person who pushed away everyone
It's my fault no one's here to wipe my tear

~

It's only me I have the right to blame
Stupid me, who couldn't put out the flame
That ate me inside has anger or hidden misery as name
It's my fault for taking the impossible as an aim

~

I am the one responsible
For everything happening to me
But isn't change still plausible?
I will get up from my own debris

~

Oh life, take this as my guarantee
I won't wait for you, I will set myself free

============

2. A Happy Ending

============

A happy, successful ending
That's all I am after
But I am an ace at blending
And causing a damn disaster

~

Oh god, what even is this world?
All my insecurities and anxieties get unfurled

~

What is my life's ultimate goal?
It certainly isn't social media's endless scroll

~

I am oh so confused
Don't we stupid teens get a mentor?
My heart and confidence are battered and bruised
Of every earthquake, I am somehow the epicenter

~

A happy ending
Sprinkled with success
My broken heart mending
Banishing stress

Is it too much to ask for?
My broken faith, can't you restore?

I know I am foolish and maybe pathetic
Though I suck at arithmetic, I sure am poetic

Are my dreams too childish and immature?
Will I be better off if I go with the flow?
These failures I should ignore or endure?
Shall I follow the tradition or step out of the shadow?

A happy and satisfactory ending
Will I see it just in my dreams?
From everyone, my dreams I am sick of defending
Am I right for going to the extremes?

Oh god, why don't you answer?
The questions I am screaming at the top of my lungs
Am I being a foolish rebel or a chancer?
My happy ending will get destroyed by the thousand
criticizing tounges

To the foolish hobbies or the right dreams am I tending?
Oh god, will I ever get what I dreamt of - My happy ending?

============

3. A Vicious Cycle

============
Why can't I be like them?
Happy and only one thing to care for
Why am I cursed to be numb?
Depression does affect my score

~

I used to be the one at the top
Now, I look at the one there
My crown, they made me drop
I was still giving it my best, I swear

~

Work triggers depression, which in turn triggers work
Broken, forgotten, in the shadows, alone I lurk
It's a vicious cycle, viruses corrupting the whole network

~

My efforts didn't even flicker
I was pushing myself all along
Maybe, they were quicker
I know it's right, but it feels so wrong

~

The winners keep changing
This is how the world works
When my trophies, I was arranging
He made his way to the perks

~

I hand over my crown, smiling, then, cry myself to sleep
How can a medicine like time heal a cut so deep?
Caught in a vicious cycle, now all I can do is weep

~

I know I shouldn't feel bad
He worked harder and nailed it
But efforts flowing in the drain make me mad
Leave me questioning my own wit

~

Saying "I am happy for you" is easy
Congratulations on defeating a kid fighting two wars
She lost to the stormy winds, you won with the breezy
No doubt, the honor, the crown, should be yours

~

Losing because I was dejected, dejected because I lost
Overlooked winning to fight losing, now I pay the cost
Was nailing as well, before my way, this vicious cycle
crossed...

=============

4. Fake Regrets

============

Just to talk it out was all I needed
But you were always too busy
Fake regrets, weeping, why I proceeded
Your Hypocrisy makes me dizzy

~

You ask what you could have done?
Maybe not devoiding my life of fun
Maybe not treating me like everyone
Maybe actually treating me like a son

~

A simple hug
Or a gentle pat
Champagne we chug
Have a nice chat

~

And I wouldn't have done something so major
My story wouldn't have been titled 'Grievances of a Teenager'
My feelings wouldn't have been limited to only a pager
If your actions didn't scream 'I just want to cage her!'

~

Oh all your fake regrets
Still make my blood boil
All of your brutal threats
Forcing me to toil and toil

~

You knew it all very well from the start
Your actions were piercing my heart
You still didn't stop, tore me apart
Now you continue fake regrets, acting so smart

~

Some care was all I asked
But maybe it was too much
Probably my fault is this ghost of the past
I am to blame when I flinch at your touch

~

My fault, I couldn't be one of your assets
My fault, you harmed yourself with cigarettes
So I punished myself, Why do you cry for what this girl gets?
If it all was my fault, then...why do you pretend to drown in
these fake regrets?

=============

5. How Long Will It Hurt?

============
How long will it hurt?
Feels like you have shot a bullet through my heart
Why did you desert?
After knowing you were the one keeping me from falling
apart

~

Now there is no one to hug me tight
To rub my back, saying it will be alright
Teaching me to live every single night
Daily, filling my heart with delight

~

Now I wipe my tears as I come undone
Fake smiles, all it takes to fool everyone
You were the only one they couldn't outrun
But now people calling out my bluff have again turned to
none

~

How long will it hurt?
I can feel myself fall apart

Sobbing into your shirt
Inhaling comfort, trying my best to outsmart my heart

~

Tricking my brain into thinking it's you I am with
As I hug my pillow, mumbling love is a myth
And feel the pain make my stupid heart writhe
I open another bottle of wine while being on my fifth

~

I cry myself to sleep while cursing your name
Screaming about how love is a losing game
As my heart burns in the flame of blame
I would do everything only if you, I could reclaim

~

How long will it hurt?
With you, I lost my own part
I am still on the outskirt
Where you first called me sweetheart

~

I watched the sun set and rise while knowing it's getting late
Thinking how seeing your name flash on my phone would be
great
I can't breathe let alone sleep when we are separate
My heart versus mind, tired of listening to this endless debate

~

You are gone forever, I make my mind alert
Bury my feelings and tears under layers of dirt
Till when will I feel this disconcert?

Oh god, how long will it hurt?

============

6. Our Broken Vow

============
How?
I don't know
Vow
To which I should've said no
Now
My life is a mere show

~

Why did I trust when my past warned me not to?
Why did I come heartbroken back to you?
Why I believed that horrible bluff to be a vow that too true?

~

I held your hand
Looked into your eyes
Love slipped like sand
Now, my senses do arise

~

How?
I should've known
Vow
Along with my faith is blown

Now

I bleed from cuts to the bone

~

Why did I belive in your 'All will be well'?

How did I not see through your spell?

How could I belive your hand would pull me out of this hell?

~

I guess you didn't mean a word

Of all the promises we made

Now, I see, we together were absurd

You were bound to rain on my parade

~

How?

I thought I was smart

Vow

That later tore my heart

Now

I lock myself alone and fall apart

~

We both made promises of forever together

But your heart changed like the weather

How can my heart be heavy as a weeping cloud and yours as

light as a feather?

~

Every second ringing in my ear

Are your false vows I fell for

'Love is a myth' says my every tear

I am left wishing my waves had never met your shore

~

How?

Can time heal a cut so deep?

Vow

That we both failed to keep

Now

My faith is in an eternal sleep

~

To forget you, forget us, will my heart ever allow?

Will I ever recover from my broken trust, our broken vow?

=============

7. Leave Me Alone

============

Please leave me alone
I will only bring hurt
Leave me on my own
Sobbing into my shirt

~

I am made this way
I will make your life, like mine, cliche
My world of darkness can't be driven away
By, oh sunshine, your single ray
So, please go without delay
With you, I am not selfish enough to stay

~

Leave me alone to my inner ghosts
They are quite hungry for more hosts
Seeing me weeping, they raise their toasts
I can't hide from them or dodge all their outposts
They won't let me come out of this ocean, guarding all coasts

~

I have accepted the inevitable, please you do too
Leave me alone to suffer through and through

From my ashes, you can make yourself a tattoo
But till then, leave me alone, my survival chances are few
Please, you don't have any idea of what you are getting
yourself into

~

Here the darkness engulfs every single hope
This race won't give you any time to think or cope
It shows a billion bad things acting like a kaleidoscope
When you think you have seen all, dread greets you with a
nope
Life is a passionate greedy hunter and you a hopeless
antelope

~

So please leave me alone
Cause my love is true
A million cuts to the bone
I will choose over hurting you...

============

8. Bottled-up Feelings

============

Bottled-up feelings explode
And cause a big blast
I am forced off the road
About to break at last

I kept all this inside me
Buried it under my tears' sea
Now the bottle has broken, setting it all free

I thought they had died
Feelings of dread, leaving me teary-eyed
To move on, I swear I tried

I assumed it would be normal again
Now, this sudden dread and anger, I fail to explain
You are confused, seeing me crying over spilled Champagne

Bottled-up feelings explode
You can't justify my reaction
Suddenly, another depressive episode?

Weeping in a scene full of action

~

You don't seem to be able to justify
Why for rain, I am cursing at the sky
Or why I am avoiding your eye
Cause all along I have been telling a lie

~

To you and myself as well
With these emotions which I am scared to tell
I assumed it was over, we had bid a farewell
But...I was just daydreaming of heaven in hell

~

Now small things are leaving me devastated
Just one failed try and I am so frustrated
A simple gesture leaves me so irritated
Regretting when I drank my tears and acted elated

~

Bottled-up feelings explode
You end up thinking I am insane
Sobbing alone, writing another ode
Done bursting with emotions, life suddenly turns mundane
again

~

Swinging from going numb to extreme rages
All because of these emotions I have bottled up for ages

=============

9. Growing Up

============

As a kid, I was scared of ghosts
Now afraid of myself that I am older
Suffocated by the way everyone boasts
To cry on I have no one's but my shoulder

~

Growing up changed to breaking down
Feeling suffocated in this so-called 'hometown'
Weeping and then crumbling like ashes on the ground

~

Who said growing up was fun?
My mind daily tells me to give up
Supporters, I have none
I pushed them away in a blowup

~

Growing up showed me life's worst side
In my room, I just want to hide
From expectations and my disappointed guide

~

How can a confident kid
Turn into an insecure teen?

Repenting everything I did
I am pathetic, I have seen

~

I know I am doing everything wrong
But in vain trying to improve all along
Thinking how this broken person used to be so damn strong

~

Growing up changed me altogether
And this change isn't for good
Mind as delicate and light as a feather
Unable to change when I know I should

~

Thinking about the future makes me panic
My confidence and dreams sink like titanic
My inner demons are very satanic

~

When I look in the mirror
I flinch at the close-up
Thinking failure is my final career
I kept on losing myself as I grew up

============

10. Perfectly Fine

============

How can you be perfectly fine?
After cutting me to the core
Pain doesnt dull even with wine
I am crying my eyes out but what for?

~

The promises that you didn't keep
Or the time you held me, allowed to weep
Regrets of why I let you cut me so deep
Or longing for a hug and to dreamlessly sleep

~

If you are the one to blame
Why is my heart burning in this flame?

~

How can you be perfectly fine?
Showing up smiling at my door
We had always walked a very thin line
Then, what am I even crying for?

~

You didn't love me and never will
The hollow promises you never tried to fill

Do you have a heart cause this kind of acting sure is a skill
How do you have the audacity to say 'It was just for a thrill' ?

~

How did I love someone like you, I am a moron
But...why do I miss you now that you are long gone?

~

How can you be perfectly fine?
After we bid a final farewell at the shore
I didn't lose just you but my life's shine
Shall I tell you all this, but what for?

~

Just for you to take my heart and stomp on it
Once again, kill me daily, bit by bit
Show affection via an adorable chit
Then, leaving only a note of 'Its over. I quit'

~

I remember sliding down the wall, reading it, screaming
He would never. This isn't from him. I must be dreaming

~

How can you be perfectly fine?
As if you didn't stab my back in the war
Be honest, were you ever mine?
If not, then, what am I even mourning for?

~

You are shining, leaving me shattered
But I am not crying because I am bruised and battered

~

You are perfectly fine after loosing a well-wisher, a true lover
While I am mourning the loss of a traitor undercover

============

11. One Word

```
============
```

Your one single word
My world comes crashing down
You are so absurd
Always stepping on my gown
First hailing me, then...snatching my crown

~

Why do you have to rain on my parade
Every goddamn time?
Tell me

~

Your tongue slits my heart like a blade
Sobbing became a pastime
And nightmares reality

~

With just a word
You burn my paradise to the ground
And what's that I heard?
Now you wish to turn the tables around
After smirking while seeing me drown

~

You think a sorry can change it all
But you are no god
Things don't work that way

~

You taught me to build the wall
The hard way by a fraud
But my pain can't just go away

~

It sure was just one word
But that doesn't dull the hurt
You, I had always preferred
But now you can't revert
Our love is lost underneath the dirt

~

Of the grave that you dug
For you, me
And our 'All is well'

~

For me, you were a drug
Falsehoods hiding reality
Your one word broke that spell

=============

12. Creeping Anxiety

============

Anxiety is creeping in
I am just a bundle of nerves with skin

⁓

Feels like I am dying
But I know am not
Time isn't frozen but flying
As I lay limp on the cot

⁓

Adrenaline surging throughout me
As if I am drowning in a sea
Trembling like the wings of a bee
As if it were zero-degree
When in reality, I am sitting in the shade of a tree

⁓

Anxiety is slowly creeping in
Whispers at 3 AM 'Let the games begin'

⁓

Gives me a surge of strength
That I didn't want midnight
My insecurities know no length

My future doesn't seem bright

~

My mind out of the blue works in light years
Goes to the memories that only bring tears
Sudden cues are triggering my mind's gears
Impossible horrible things added to the list of fears
Any common sense that's left disappears

~

Anxiety is creeping in
Tags along depression, it's lonely twin

~

One says 'They are making fun of you'
The other says, 'For that, they need to care'
Meanwhile, I scream neither is true
Engulfs my screams, wrecked despair

~

Both their claims make me deaf like dead
I lay motionless, listening, on my bed
In the end, I am the one who is misled
Thinking there is only dread
I have on my way ahead

~

Anxiety is creeping in
My self-confidence is tossed in a bin

~

All that remains in self doubt
That kills my unfinished dream

Defeated, I go down another route
Still my anxiety doesn't forget to scream

~

My heart beats fast and my chest heavs up and down
My hormones love to mess around
Feels as if, I am stuck in a countdown
That will turn zero any second, laughing will be the town
As usual, I will somehow end up being the clown

~

So judgemental and hypocritic is our society
The root cause of my lurking and creeping anxiety

=============

13. I Am Sorry

============

I am sorry
I feel guilty
What else can I say?

~

This night is starry
Crying until tea
How else can I display?

~

I really meant it when I said
I had the best of intentions
Laying on the bed, drowning in dread
Cursing all the interventions

~

I hurt you without meaning to
Things change, and control is outside your range

~

I didn't think the tables would turn
Didn't know this was where it lead
With mistakes, lessons I learn
Heal the relationships that bled

~

I am sorry

I mean it

I meant no harm

~

Riding a doomed safari

Wanna quit

Will you still hold my arm?

~

Did I break the trust we had?

Like I ruin all good things

If so, please don't be sad

My heart should be and is the one which stings

~

I swear, a fake smile I wear

As guilt emotion drowns me like an ocean

~

I am the one to blame, I confess

You had no fault in any of this

I wish that your lows are less

My punishment is this dark abyss

~

I am sorry

Please forgive

Give me punishment of choice

~

I will be chary

Learn to live

I swear I will never raise my voice

============

14. Hating Him

============

Never thought that I could
Hate someone this much
Can't forgive when I know I should
But my skin still burns from his touch

~

As a child, never thought I would say this
But even if *he* dies, him, I won't miss
I won't show empathy if he rots in the same abyss
Instead I might sigh with satisfaction of revenge and bliss

~

They say forgiveness is a nice thing to do
We will talk when you walk a mile in my shoe
And you too survive what all I struggled through
When you like me, see past the sweet lie, the bitter reality
that's true

~

Now they all see the hatred only
But never the reason that made me this way
He was never there when I was lonely
Whenever I counted on him, stabbed me, backed away

~

Now when he needs me, he remembers I have his blood in
me
How funny he doesn't know that blood doesn't make family
Love, care and support does, which he always used to oversee
Everyone expects me to forget, how he left a little girl alone,
chose to flee

~

They say I am so stone hearted to hate him with all my heart
But no one noticed when I trembled when he called me
sweetheart
How all his little actions gave my hatred such a headstart
How everyday he twisted my young mind and slowly tore me
apart

~

I cant forget then, I won't forgive
How he ruined my mental state
My blood will boil on seeing him till I live
Whenever I see him, all I feel will be hate

============

15. Becoming Numb

============

When did I become
To everything, so numb?
Don't even try to overcome
The thoughts that say I am scum

~

Whether you scream at me or hug me tight
The only thing I feel is lost in this eternal night
I don't feel like waiting or searching for light
I feel nothing at all, may it be pain or delight
But I promise, faking a smile, I will be alright

~

You tell me to talk it out
But I wanna be alone
On you, I don't have a doubt
I just feel like I have a heart of stone

~

My heart is shattered and broken
But I can't feel anything at all
Feelings are in a deep sleep, still haven't woken
It seems I am transparent and oh-so-small

~

I can't feel anything, I don't react
It's like my brain refuses to feel the impact
My mind has malfunctioned, and my feelings have blacked
All these negative thoughts I strongly attract
I feel like ending mine and life's pact

~

When did burying my emotions
Become a rule of thumb?
When did I stop caring about demotions
And become to everything so numb...?

=============

16. I And Him

<pre>============</pre>

Why am I cursed
To be stuck with him?
My emotions burst
In my mind, these thoughts swim

If he cannot die
Then please kill me
When he meets my eye
Vanishes every trace of glee

Anger fills my heart to the top
A thousand sad flashbacks pop
Making me remember that drop
That close call on the rooftop
While I beg my mind to stop

This torture is unbearable
Why shouldn't I end it all?
To me, life has always been terrible
Why shall I wait for the next fall?

~

I can't stand him anymore
He made me go through hell
He was supposed to be my mentor
But always laughed when I fell

~

Why is he still with me?
This unfair fate is so funny
Oh so dark, this reality
Alone, you need to rise from your debris
Need to follow the verdict of a biased referee

~

Why can't he leave forever
Or let me go away?
Plots schemes and acts clever
Plays the victim for a clean display

~

I and him
We used to be strong
When times turned grim
He just played along

~

Acted supportive, then left in a snap
Stupid me got stuck in his trap
Forced me to go through all this crap
Now he wonders why there is this gap
Between us, wants to cover it ASAP

But the spark between us has turned dim
Now we are separated forever I and him...

============

17. Love Is So Stupid

<pre>
============
</pre>

I don't know why you affect me
I swear I no longer care
I knew all along you would flee
Stupid little hopes steepen the slopes

~

Love is so stupid and cruel
Curse you, Cupid, made me a fool

~

I don't know why or how
But I fell hard for you
Knew it was a false vow
What have I gotten myself into?

~

You have taken up my mind
Love really makes you blind
I thought we were intertwined
Beloved you, a wicked mastermind

~

Love is stupid and oh-so-rough
Curse you Cupid, and your sweet bluff

~

I wish I had control over myself
When you said only I was in your view
While putting that tragic book on the shelf
And making my life one too

~

I have lost my identity and sense
I know you lost things as well
Now, we together aren't comfy but tense
It's hard to live and hard to bid farewell

~

Love is so stupid and misleading
Curse you cupid, two hearts are bleeding

~

It's so hard to see the bed not messed
And to return your shirts that I stole
But so is with you, being obsessed
To glance at you, and lose all control

~

Still, you are the only one I think of
I know you too are cursing the cupid above
For both of us, patching and breaking seem tough
Oh so confusing and stupid is love

=============

18. Coming Back Again

============

Why do I keep coming back to you?
When I know it will just bring hurt
Why can't I remove you from my view?
When I know, in the end, me, you will desert

~

I know you are going to pierce my heart
With that large ego of yours
Slowly or fast, you will tear me apart
Hit me in the face with a billion wars

~

Still, I come back
So that you can hurt me more
Warns me, a flashback
But I still let you cut me to the core

~

Coming back again
Such a foolish deed
Choking on this pain
Am I alive only to bleed?

~

Why can't I leave once and for all
End this godforsaken dread
Why don't I too drown myself in alcohol
Why do I embrace you instead?

~

Love is so stupid
It ends all senses
Curse you damned Cupid
For making me face all the consequences

~

I know all this
Still, I come back, why?
For ages rotting in an abyss
But still dreaming about the sky

~

I always come back, don't I?
Times when I don't regret this are few
You melt my heart with the 'I love you' lie
But we both know, I will still come back to you

=============

19. Stop This Mind Twisting

Stop this mind-twisting
Depression already is a losing game
These dark thoughts, I try resisting
But you make it harder with every claim

You always say I pretend when I cry
Might say the exact same when I die
Kill myself without saying goodbye
Then you will ask my lifeless body why?

Oh god, why can't you see?
How much you have broken me
Mental abuse is your cup of tea
This gaslighting makes me lose reality
Unaffected, you throw away my trust's debris

Like it's nothing but lose trash
You burned my remains in a flash
Still I rose from that very ash

That you sold for some cash
Like this, my mind will crash

~

Can't you stop this mind-twisting?
My life on its own is a losing game
I no longer feel like existing
In a world that knows me by your name

~

I have tried so hard to erase my past
Developed traits, you that contrast
We might share a similar face and caste
And a hell lot of time might have passed
But I am no longer the way I came out of your molded cast

~

Why don't you give up on your goal?
To daily painfully shatter my soul
From my heart, you have blasted a hole
I don't wanna be under your control
Stop twisting my mind in the name of console

~

I am fighting myself every day and every night
Still, I am failing to make things right
I am sick of mending my heart after your every smight
Sick of lying to myself and whispering 'It's alright...'
Stop dragging me back when I am crawling towards the light

~

Stop this mind-twisting
And yelling that I am to blame
With you, it's hard coexisting
When you treat my life and feelings like a game

=============

20. A Billion Little Thoughts

============

One single mind
A billion little thoughts
Always on the grind
One after other shots

~

My mind is clouded
I don't know anything
Yet I know it all

~

This place is so crowded
So full of everything
Yet I feel lonely and small

~

A million thoughts, revolting to get attention
None of them are appropriate for a mention
I am afraid my neurons will burst from tension

~

Plug in earphones, getting high on songs
Drowning these voices, forgetting the wrongs

My mind seems to be the place, where all the darkness
belongs

~

I am scared yet positive
And happy yet sad
All at the same time

~

These thoughts are causative
I might go from numb to mad
The thing keeping me sane is a rhyme

~

One person, so many dreams
Personalities I have got lots and lots
So many views with different schemes and themes
How can a single mind handle a billion thoughts?

============

21. An Unspoken Vow

============

Guess it will never ever end
Maybe it is a part of me now
Guess I can never ever blend
Maybe hidden in my past is an unspoken vow

⁓

The oath to never forgive or forget
To be cold hearted when he dies of regret
For his falsehoods, to not break a sweat
To show life, I have not given up yet

⁓

The oath to bravely carry on, be it dusk or dawn
The oath to accept the flaws, be the storm's cause

⁓

How can I forget it all?
Act like everyone around
As if I didn't fall
The bitter truth of life wasn't found

⁓

By me, oh so eventful dread filled was that night
The curious mind and stupid heart's fight

When life smacked me down with all its might
And I still got up trembling to see the truth and find the
light

~

How can I expect that, over is that bloody combat?
Do all these people don't see, or unlucky was only me?

~

Why is trauma a part of me?
Can't it just go away?
I try to set myself free
But it has all of me in every way

~

This ivy is growing over my life of stone
Whispering at midnight 'You will always be alone'
And indeed I fight all of them on my own
Here not dying daily in itself is a milestone

~

I never ever wanted, to be haunted
By that oath that has filled me with self loath

~

Guess I would die in regret
Of the vow I unwillingly took
Maybe I can never ever forget
Trauma has me on its hook

~

Guess I am just a puppet tied with trauma's strings
Guess I am the fallen angel who failed to sprout wings

Maybe I can't break anyhow, that ill-fated unspoken vow

============

22. My Dark Place

============

There is a dark place
It's in my mind
After falling from grace
There refugee I find

~

It's sad, horrifying yet gives a sense of home
Don't know what to call this peculiar syndrome
Here my peace and glee love to roam
But aeons old things burn down, just like Rome
Despair surges through my heart at a billion ohm

~

Home is where the heart is indeed
Mine is in a dark pit, unfilled is every need
For some emotions, ready to beg and plead

~

There is a dark place
It's in my mind
Darkness, I embrace
Life can never be kind

~

I try to crawl out and run towards the light
However the most I can do is put up a good fight
I am again tossed in this dark and eternal night
It makes me forget the sensation of delight
I am left questioning if in my life anything is right

~

I hate it, I love it, I hate that I love it so much
Happiness turns to dread with my mere touch
Weird but I have found home in darknes's clutch

~

There is a dark place
It's in my mind
When I get sick of this race
I turn around and look behind

~

At everything that crumbled in front of my eyes
I cover my ears as the voices in my head rise
'You belong here, stay with us' They summarise
It is like the castle of Hades in heaven's disguise
It's the sorrowful tale of my faith's demise

~

I am lost in the dark but at least it doesn't feel strange
After all glee has always been out of my range
I am afraid not of this dark place but petrified of change

~

There is a dark place
It's in my mind

But it's my personal space
That too one of a kind

~

I can't leave it for I love it with all my heart
So, I will rot here untill my dark place tears me apart

=============

23. Sick Of Crying

============

I am sick of crying
Why do I still care?
Depression is undying
Says my every tear

~

My eyes have dried
Emotions are not on my side
They are swallowing my pride
Lack of water and excess of emotions inside
I am left mortified

~

I am fed up of everything
The problem is within me I know
But only more dread thoughts bring
Seems depressed, even my shadow

~

I am sick of crying
Why do I still care?
Myself, I find terrifying
Can't life be for once fair?

~

Crying makes me feel vulnerable and weak
The truth as usual, I am afraid to speak
So at midnight, out I sneak
Scream and weep on the road like a freak
At least on the road, there is a less judgemental critique

~

Maybe I am not strong enough
A crybaby is all I will ever be
But maybe my life is indeed tough
I have lost the sense of reality

~

I am sick of crying
Why do I still care?
Just when my cheeks are drying
I am again consumed by this nightmare

~

'You will never get out of this' my thoughts taunt
'You, these past trauma's will always haunt'
But being normal and happy is my only want
Maybe chatting and laughing with friends at a restaurant
But pushed from the peak, now I am lying broken on the
Piedmont

~

Shall I still get up and fight?
'All you need to do is try'
I really am holding tight

I have had enough, I refuse to cry

============

Getting Up

To the times you got up even when you knew life would throw you down again...

To the times you showed the courage to fight yourself...

To the times you dared to confront your feelings...

To the times you stood up for yourself...

To the times you swallowed the bitter pill of betrayal and stood stronger than a mountain...

To the times you saw your castle crumble yet never gave up...

And lastly, to the times you locked yourself in your room, cried alone, and then went outside with a wide smile as if nothing happened...

YOU right there, are a warrior bedecked with battle scars, the only evidence of the war no one knew about.

24. Trying

============

Trying and trying
Failing and resorting to crying
It's like time is flying
And the pilot is not worth relying

⁓

But I look around
Try to fix the pieces in place
Again, fall down
As usual brought disgrace

⁓

To everyone
And everything
I try to fly and run
They did cut my wing

⁓

Trying sure is hard
For luck, I have no regard

⁓

Trying my best
Giving it all I have got

They say I am obsessed
But mock when I don't get the first spot

~

Mentally torturing myself
In the name of trying
Read the whole towering bookshelf
But for you, the result still wasn't satisfying

~

Trying doesn't mean attempting again
While mentally accepting defeat
It means tearing through the hurricane
Telling yourself you will win on repeat

~

The whole world can be on fire
But you should still try to find the sea
Not winning but attempting, we admire
You rising from your own debris

~

That's what trying really means
It's not an attempt but a part of your routines

~

Don't question yourself - Are you worth qualifying?
If you dared to attempt you are tough
The only thing left now is to keep trying
That attitude, my friend, is enough

============

25. Just A Human

============
I do good I am not an angel though
I do sins but I am not the devil
I am a human like the thousands that come and go
Feels like I have a merged, blurred level

~

I am a human and just that
The troops wouldn't ask where I am at
Just an irrelevant soldier in this combat

~

My character isn't white or black
But one of the shades of gray
Confused, I easily loose track
Of if I am on a good or wicked way

~

I am not a natural, have never been
I only try and cry after I begin
Have lost a million times but still wishing to win

~

I am neither the villan nor the hero
Just one of the passers by about to die

Neither a ten nor a zero
A mediocre whose cry never meets the eye

An average human and that's all
Born only to wither and fall
Someone whom after death, no one will ever recall

Then, give me chances if I am not enough
Grant me permission to fail and learn
If I am average, invest on me, make me tough
Don't go hard on me, just show some gentle concern

You are not some lifeless program
Don't be hard on yourself, little man
Excuse yourself, you are just a human the way I am

============

26. Too Late

============

When I was a kid no one was there
To hear how my day was
Now, I have learned to wipe my own tear
You say you love me and accept all my flaws
Didn't care when I drowned in despair
Now my loneliness or self sufficiency you wanna pause

~

You expect my long-lost love to arouse
Because though late, you finally feel awake
When I feel uneasy you raise your eyebrows
Cause the only language you know is give or take
Now that I don't care if anyone allows
So, you want me to put my mental health at stake

~

That too for you
The one who destroyed me
I know my trauma was true
Isn't easy, watching your only trustee flee
I remember all I suffered through
And how rose from my own debris

~

I can't erase the trauma from my brain
Just because you said you were sorry
I can't cope, can't dull the pain
Hug you while watching the night so starry
From me, now, you can't snatch the reign
Expect me to go blindfolded in your Ferrari

~

Where were you when I was in need?
Don't say you couldn't see, were you blind?
You never showed up and left me to bleed
Now you want that place in my heart, you resigned
For it, this late now, you beg and plead
Why don't you give up on twisting my mind?

~

The day I forget it, I will forgive you
Five years and still haunts me
No matter now, what you say or do
You have broken our relation beyond repair, can't you see?
No one was there to hand me a tissue
Now you want me to believe your fake guarantee

~

Some mistakes can't be corrected
Saying sorry later won't help gather this mess
You want us to still be connected
Your Hypocrisy, I just can't process
Look, my life how much you have affected

How can you still hope for this relation to be a success?

~

I know all about your Hypocrisy
Give up your dream of tricking me again
This world lives on democracy
You can't tell me what to attain
Over are the days of your aristocracy
I know what's truly behind that love's veil

~

You can't undo the crap you did
Yet want me to forgive and love you
You come after a goodbye we bid
And now say your love was true
Then, why couldn't you care for that kid?
Who had not a superhero's but your tattoo

~

You want us to reunite
Now that our lives are separate
You left me in the night for your light
Now you question why my trust is delicate
Now you want it all to be alright
But honey...now it's too late...

============

27. Life Throws Me Down

============

Life throws me down
I shatter like a vase
Try to go around
It slows my pace

~

There are memories chasing me that I wanna forget
Bitter thoughts, mistakes, and decisions that I regret
Horrors about the ones who were a scary threat
When I was so weak, vulnerable, and got so easily upset
I am running as fast as I can, drenched in sweat

~

They are catching up, my heart is pounding loud
I feel so distant and alone even in a crowd
But I will run fast and never give up, I vowed
Oh life, in this everlong road, isn't there a shroud?
Frustrated, tired, and hopeless, I thunder and rain like a
weeping cloud

~

Life throws me down
I don't fight but fall
It makes me drown
I don't try to get out at all

~

It's gonna throw me down again, what's the point in getting
up?
I am so small and weak, like, crying for his mother, a lonely
pup
I sigh, escape the labyrinth of thoughts, and shove feelings
aside, myself I pickup
I calm my mind and then, the mess you made of me, oh life,
I clean up
I take my heart, mind, fate, and feelings, all that you
crumbled like a paper cup

~

I will fight, dodge the problems, catch obstacles, throw them
back at you
I will find a way out of all problems even when you don't
give a clue
I will handle all the torture, emotional, physical, all you
subject me to
I will live to the full, even if all the happy moments you give
are few
This warrior is ready to slaughter, all the difficulties stand in a
queue!

~

It is not a hero but villain
Don't let life step on your gown
Ignore it's laugh, you should be chillin'
And laugh when life tries to throw you down

============

28. I Finally Feel Clean

I think I am finally out of it
Crawled out of the hell I was in
So thankful that I didn't quit
Persistence and dedication made me win

I finally feel clean
Only scars left that too healed
Reclaimed my position as queen
After ages of bleeding on the battlefield

I was never fond of change
But now, I know I was wrong
Change at first, might seem strange
But it has the power to make you strong

I have left the traumatic past behind
Not gonna lie, it sure was hard
Took years to get hold of my own mind
To break down the ages-old walls, lower my guard

But, I finally feel clean
Learned to live without a shield
Learned life can't be evergreen
But the injuries sure can be healed

~

You can fall from a mountain peak
And then crash straight into hell
But that doesn't label you as weak
But a great warrior with the courage to rebel

~

The dark place that bounded you with chains
Is not and can never be forever
It's still your choice, snatch those reigns
From life, Although it's clever, don't you bever

~

Then, like me, you will finally feel clean
Remember the bleeding bark is always healed
It's You versus Life no one in between
Go, sow seeds of success, and then, enjoy the yield

=============

29. Wanted Not Needed

============

Five years of surviving hell
Has taught me this
Alone, you can cry and yell
Still, pull yourself out of the abyss

~

I have realized I always wanted support
But I never needed it, a chance to stab
I am improving says my report
Alive even after facing all this crap

~

All I wish for is that
I could tell my past self some things
Stop her from screaming where is God at?
Tell her to fight when they tear her wings

~

Tell her not to tolerate any more
She is capable enough for an uproar
Those critics, she should ignore
It was a want but never a need that mentor
Your heart who ruthlessly tore

~

I never needed anyone
I always was enough
Stars aren't needed by the sun
Cause like me it's more tough

~

Wants aren't needs
I wish I knew then
One who leads
Isn't required again

~

If only anyone had told me
'You don't need to beg for help'
'You are strong enough to survive reality'
For them, I wouldn't have made a yelp

=============

30. Trauma

============

Trauma doesn't strengthen you
It breaks you bit by bit
Having no one to go to
Makes you want to quit

~

You get frustrated, why can't you just move on?
Like others, can't you forget and stop acting like a moron

~

But you overlook they weren't going through the pain
Their life, they were not struggling to maintain
So, why do you want to have like them, a smart brain?

~

Stop asking 'Why me?'
Trauma isn't choosy at all
Everyone can drown in the sea
A billionaire and a beggar both face a downfall

~

Everyone has his own personal hell
The question is how good you are at hiding it
You can make your trauma's end well

Only if you refuse to submit

~

Trauma is just a minor obstacle or an impenetrable wall
It all depends on you
You can't decline but can cushion the fall
Everything comes down to your view

~

So, break those chains of trauma
Don't forget or forgive but recover
Life is just a pointless melodrama
But you have the choice to rediscover

~

Heal that inner child, please...
It's been bleeding for ages
Promise it and you can do it with ease
Trauma is just a chapter in life's book full of pages

=============

31. A Dive

============

Its been quite a while since I felt alive
Hit my peak, failed to speak and then started to jive
Just going and flowing with water, after taking a deep dive

~

Unaffected
Just can't give a damn
Disconnected
Emotions stuck in a traffic jam

~

Feeling nothing like I am dead
Appealing to the god overhead
Dealing with only grief and dread
Kneeling to the pointless war ahead

~

Maybe it's for my own good
If I don't feel bliss, can't get hurt
I can't be misunderstood
If I leave all this and dare to desert

~

They say everything happens for good
What on earth is the point then?
Why to sacrifice joy for falsehood
If I won't feel anything ever again?

~

To taste the holy drops of bliss
I am ready to pay struggle as a price
About sweet times, I reminisce
When I felt both bad and nice, it was paradise

~

What if it's been a while since I felt alive?
Hit a peak, a dip broke my streak but I did revive
I won't go with the flow of water but bring a tsunami, make
every wave remember that dive
And watch how even on the seabed a rebel can thrive

============

Short Poems

This is for all the poem lovers out there. People like me who can't start their day without their daily dose of rhymes and soul-touching thoughts. People who are aware of the magic words trap within the rhymes. Most of the poems in this section are barely ten lines long because I understand that it can be hard to squeeze time out of the sophisticated schedule we all have.

So, enjoy the short poems with heavy doses of rhymes, emotions, and rebellious ideas in them...

32. Pawn

============

Oh honey, was I just a pawn?
In a game of feelings that you played
Maybe, it was dusk, not dawn
Just a faint attraction, bound to fade

~

I treated you like a king but you treated me like a game
Now, you simply turn the tables, pushing me into the flame
of blame

~

You knew I was all alone
With no shoulder to cry upon
Still dared to snatch my throne
But forgot, a queen can spawn from a pawn

============

33. Historical

<pre>
============
</pre>

The battle of you and me
It will be a historical scene
It's inevitable, we both agree
Now, no one can intervene

~

The war of a blind believer and a traitor
The bruised and his stinging scar's creator

~

To see the whole world going up in flames
I don't need to be an Oracle
The future will remember our names
As the leaders of a war so historical

<pre>
============
</pre>

34. Tranquil

============

She looks so tranquil on the surface, doesn't she?
But her eyes are hiding a storm
She has a habit of rising from her own debris
Doesn't need you, knows how to keep herself warm

~

She is the black sky, ready to weep
But has buried her emotions down deep
For your safety, don't poke the lioness who is asleep

============

35. Penalty

============

You made me go through hell
Forgot the penalty? Now, get ready to pay
Neither was all nor the end will be well
Now the tables have turned, you are my prey

~

Run, karma is coming to get you
None of your promises were true
The scar you gave me is like a tattoo
It's a reminder to extract the penalty that's due

============

36. Sophisticated

============

You see me right where you left me
Standing alone, feeling alienated
But darling, this is my cup of tea
I have always been isolated
The scars on my back that you see
Have made me this sophisticated

~

I was ready for the blow
Knew it, me, you would try to deceive
All who you knew was my shadow
Honey, I am sophisticated, not naive

============

37. Legendary

Oh honey, our battle will be legendary
I tried for peace, avoided it for ages
But now, you have made it necessary
The story isn't over, left are a couple hundred pages

Remember, this was what you wanted
By that December, you will be haunted
Like an ember, you will burn and feel daunted

This will be a fully planned war, nowhere near arbitrary
The world will get consumed by the raging flames of this
war...Oh honey, it will be legendary...

38. Construct

============

It's so easy to construct
The building called house
But when the petals are plucked
A glorious rose becomes a louse

~

Without love, it can't become a home
It remains a lifeless building
Looks so beautiful with that dome
But that beauty is only the gilding

~

It's not a home but a house, if out, love is sucked
If you have a heart of stone, a home, you can never construct

============

39. Banish

==============

You were everything to me
I am banished, seeing you go
You said you are letting me free
But I feel banished, why don't you know?

~

I am in exile, you were my town
Once in a while, please promise to come around
Together, we will walk a mile, I will carry your crown
I want to see you smile, I will ease your frown

~

When did the love, trust, and magic vanish?
You said you loved me, then, me, why did you banish?

==============

40. Language

The language that you taught me
For only us to understand
Is concealed beneath the debris
Of our love's forgotten land

~

I can't speak it with anyone else and I am craving those sweet
words
No one else captures me in their embrace while listening to
the birds

~

I am dying to hear the words from you
Missing the gentle kisses on the cheek
Now, weeping, I am kissing your name's tattoo
Cursing the language we both used to speak

41. Society

=============

Our society
Such a funny thing
Loves variety
Yet tears every sprouting wing

~

Says girls can't fight and boys can't cook
Yet the gender of the knight wasn't written in any book

~

Mocks everyone for every mistake
Then wonders 'What is anxiety?'
Someone shares pain, it labels them as fake
We don't need to give a damn about such a society

=============

42. Ambition

============

Oh these stupid ambitions

So damn powerful and strong

Don't care about conditions

Or if they and expectations get along

~

Dreaming big is harmful yet so addicting

Both our views can be right yet conflicting

~

Haunted by the ghost of failing

Bounded by permissions

Still, little dreams are prevailing

Why is enduring pain the cost of ambitions...?

============

43. Eruption

============

This eruption of emotions
Always gets the best of me
Tired of coping with demotions
And faking glee, rising from my own debris

~

I am drowning in my thoughts, choking on my feelings
Tired of joining the dots, every night, 2 AM staring
dead-eyed at the ceiling

~

Another depressive episode
Such a rude interruption
The only coping method - an ode
For gathering myself after this eruption

============

44. Sailor

============

I am the sailor of my ship of dreams
Stop manipulating my mind with your stupid schemes
You might be a prism but I won't bend like other beams

~

It's my life
And my rules
I will dodge your rife
I am not like other fools

~

Of a million forgotten dreams, you might be the jailor
Seeing you, the most confident ones might turn paler and
paler
But I am not a slave to be packed in this ship, honey, I am
the sailor

============

45. Veil

The door to my soul has been veiled
It's for my own protection
The ship of trust sank every time it sailed
Not very trusting but craving affection

~

Why shall I make others worry about a problem not
bothering them?
Let me hide my tears behind a veil, and hug the people I
condemn

~

Got betrayed, every time I trusted
So sorrow-filled is my tale
With humanity, I feel disgusted
So, I just hide behind a veil

46. Memory

My memory is filled with pain
I guess some scars never heal
Efforts to forget are all in vain
Hopelessness becomes all I feel

~

I can't relive the same trauma, don't you get it, my stupid
mind?
I just want to reset my memory, leave all these issues behind

~

I am so broken and bruised
But I always say, "Don't worry. I am fine"
After all this, I just feel used
Why can't you learn to forget, stupid memory of mine?

47. Provoke

============

Don't provoke this secretive little girl
If you dare, then, a hidden beast will unfurl

~

Her eyes are hiding a storm
And her sleeves, battle scars
Revenge makes her heart warm
With Lucifer himself, she is at pars

~

She has risen from her own ashes
Wears smoke like a cloak
Never seen again, with her who clashes
The ruthlessness isn't dead if not awoke, the fallen angel,

don't provoke

============

Special Bonus

These poem are dedicated to all the people who struggle to express their emotions and prefer bottling them up...

For the people who always say - 'I am fine' when they really are not...

For the people who try their best but still are never enough for others...

For the people who have their arms bedecked with scars...

For the people who are still haunted by the ghost of their pasts even after desperate attempts to forget...

For the people who always overlook their interests and end up hurting themselves with their selfless behaviour...

For the people who were so busy being strong, that they forgot to be happy...

These poems are a gentle reminder, a beautifully true message for especially YOU, buddy.

48. Time To Let Go

============

Oh, buddy, It's time to let go
This weight will make you drown
Allow your emotions to flow
Staying attached to your Hut will make you lose the crown

~

Trust me, I know it's hard
Those memories are close to your heart
Your past, I don't tell you to disregard
But you shouldn't let that trauma tear you apart

~

You think your sufferings are concealed
But I see you bleeding on the battlefield

~

Oh buddy it's time to let go
This weight will make you drown
You can and will win, we both know
But not with your past stepping on your gown

~

I am not telling you to forget
Cause I know that can't happen

But don't let it make you upset
Overcome that unfair misshapen

~

You might have walked alone through hell but smiled for the
world
But mate, don't you let that inner unhealed child get
unfurled

~

Oh buddy, it's time to let go
This weight will make you drown
You might have gone down with a blow
Yet stood strong to fool the entire town

~

You have learned your lesson now
Stop torturing yourself with flashbacks
Even a farmer puts down the heavy plough
The woodcutter washes away the guilt, lowers the axe

~

It's time to step out of the dark shadow
Buddy, it's over...It's time to let go...

=============

49. No Need To Be Perfect

There is no need to be perfect
Oh love, you are enough
Stop changing the subject
Whenever you are asked if you are rough and tough

~

You have always given your best
Worked from dusk till dawn
Buddy, you need some rest
From one after another moron

~

Telling you you are a failure and a waste of space
Screaming how you have always only brought disgrace
The one who always says your mind is not in place
Oh buddy, they are mere obstacles trying to slow your pace
Cause they themselves never won with life, this race

~

There is no need to be perfect
Oh love, you are enough
Imperfection is an aspect

Of being a human - the hub of bluff

~

You can't ever satisfy or shut people up
The past gives evidence of the same
It's fine to drink on the moonlit roof from a plastic cup
It's fine if not everybody knows your name

~

You cant undevelop yourself to be the one they like
It's like tumbling down after an hour long hike
And chasing an aeroplane with a mountain bike
They will hate you again if you miss one single strike
Do you want to be the one whose persona and person are
nothing alike?

~

Why do you wanna be perfect?
Oh love, you are enough
You are a human not an object
You don't need to be tough

=============

50. Your False Smile

<pre>
============
</pre>

Your false smile
And secrets untold
Faith in exile
You still will be bold

~

I know, you know, we both know that
Where are your concealed scars at?
Are you still hiding the only evidence of that combat?

~

I hope you win the war
You told no one about
Hope they heal, the cuts to the core
The medicine, I know, you will soon figure out

~

Your false smile
And secrets untold
Complicated, your file
Kind-hearted yet cold

~

Till when will you hide it all?
Alone gather yourself after every fall?
Till when will you withhold that wall?

~

You might be safe behind them
But are you happy for true?
Do you really want to eradicate the mayhem
And live alone with your baseless taboo?

~

Your false smile
And secrets untold
Scares Satan, Your profile
The secrets and power you hold

~

Drop that smile because you are free to cry
Scream the bitter truth, stop cherishing the sweet lie
The tears you don't let slip, rain down heavily from the
weeping sky

~

Your sealed lips don't say much
But your silence says it all
Your life is a victim of Midas' touch
Looks bright from the outside but is a tragic tale of downfall

~

Your false smile
And secrets untold
Change your lifestyle

For enough time, you have been bold

After reading your mind, honey, I am in tears
Please stop...You don't need to be the one, a false smile who
wears...

============

About The Author

DrishKing or Drishti Ummat is a high schooler with a burning passion for writing books. She is a true bookworm, always trying to read as many books as possible. Somehow, that high schooler got interested in writing books. Her love for writing fuels her self-publishing. She is an introvert who despises reality and lives in her own world, which is filled with horrors, mystery, and humor.

Although not published, she has written quite a few books and is slowly editing and publishing them as e-books, paperbacks, hardcovers, and everything else you can ask for.

She currently lives with her family in Bathinda, Punjab.

The author can be contacted via -

E-mail: drishtiummat@gmail.com

Books By The Author

Midnight Poetry: Dark Poems With Concealed Motivation

Life isn't a bed of roses but more like a Ferris wheel. Ups and downs are an inevitable part of life. At times, one might ask himself why he should get up after a fall when all that is waiting for him is misery and more obstacles to face. At those times, he needs to get up and stand as strong as a mountain, ready to embrace the upcoming difficulties like a warrior.

This poem collection having fifty hand-picked poems explores the dark thoughts one might get in such hard times and help him to get up after every blow of life. These dark poems with concealed motivation enlighten issues that you might relate to or might be suffering through. Relating to a piece of writing and getting a sense of being understood when you think that you are the only one suffering can do wonders on a mind drowning in negativity.

'Not too many things feel greater than being understood'

And a poem is a thing that can be enjoyed by multiple people with different likings. From an old person to a little kid, we all enjoy reciting poems.

Guilty Or Not...?: Secrets Of A Wanted Criminal

Will justice be served to all the families he had destroyed or to the family he was desperate to make?

CIA Officer Hannah Gorgin, the most skilled in her field, is working on a case involving the murder of Henry Spark alongside her engineer brother, Frank, who is fascinated by her work. The investigation leads the unusual duo to the infamous assassin Soovin Cooper, the only criminal Hannah has been unable to put behind bars.

However, when Hannah discovers Soovin's secret, she questions his guilt. This realization causes Hannah to reevaluate her feelings towards Soovin, and she even contemplates leaving her life behind to be with the pseudo-assassin and a little girl.

She finds herself torn between her duty and her emotions.

But the question remains - Is Soovin truly ready to leave his violent past behind? Furthermore, is this all a mere sinister plot for him or something deeper? And most importantly - Is Soovin guilty or not...?

The White Face Man: Horrors Of A Mirror

What will you do when you don't see your reflection in the mirror and are instead presented with a heart-stopping murder that will give you never-ending nightmares? Moreover, it ends with a message written in blood - 'YOU ARE NEXT'

The White Face Man isn't the devourer of just one soul. His victims push others into this whirlpool in hopes of escaping but The White Face Man shows no mercy and slaughters everyone.

"I am Cari Hallen, one of his victims. I remember thinking I had escaped as well This is my encounter with The White Face man. Lucky are the ones who haven't witnessed his horrors. Beware, now, whenever you see a mirror, you will recall a white mask and a blood-stained knife."

But can an emotionless being like The White Face Man be humane too? After all a villain is just a victim whose story hasn't been told, right?

The Curse Of KV-62: Provoking The Boy King

This is the story of -
A troubled past and a lethal curse,
A burning passion for tombs and a thousand little secrets,
Hunger for answers and an impossible mystery to solve,
Courage to break a centuries-old curse and a promise to keep with the last breath

A renowned archaeologist and Egyptologist, Ken Hudson, the tomb of Tutankhamun or KV-62, and the curse of the boy king.

After seven years of research on tombs, Ken Hudson finally got the opportunity to scrutinize the tomb of Tutankhamun, or KV 62 with his friend Clark Limberdon. He has already lost his father to the same tomb but has plucked up the courage to unveil the mystery behind his father's demise and the tomb's rumored curse.

However, when he comes across a spine-chilling, dark, prophetic note written by his father for him about the tomb, his objectives change. Now, instead of just finding the secret room in KV 62 he has been given the responsibility to uncover, he is going to cross the line and provoke the ancient forces.

Little did he know that The Tomb Of Tutankhamun was ready to take another life with it.

Join Ken Hudson in his magical adventure in The Tomb Of Tutankhamun, fighting the curse of KV-62.

Detective Wilbur Horace: A Case That Changed His Life

Detective Wilbur Horace - a detective with a little secret- is caught between three murders. The killer is overconfident for a reason, he is a true mastermind. Words like genius define him. He is leaving behind hints in the form of notes for the detective to catch up with his intelligence. But Wilbur Horace is a mastermind himself and he is the only one who can match the intelligence of the killer.

In fact, he is similar to the killer in countless ways, with similar habits, similar styles, and even the same blood group.

Will Wilbur be able to uncover the mystery behind the killings while hiding his little secret...? Will the killer get away with all the three murders he has committed? Or will Wilbur be able to decode the clues left behind, and put him behind bars? Or will this case take an unexpected turn so that neither of that happens, both of them lose and both of them somehow win in this face-off...?

Join Detective Wilbur on this case to find out...

A True Mastermind-JJ: What Happens When An Author Has To Save Not A Character's Life But Her Own?

It had been really easy to put my book's characters into lethal situations and take risks that could either end their lives or save them, but trust me, it's a lot more difficult to make such decisions when life at sake isn't of a fictional character, but yours.

I am a successful crime-fiction author, Jamie Jennifer or JJ, as I am usually called. I lead a pretty normal life. My biggest problem can be a deadline for work but nothing more serious until a psycho killer kidnaps me and wants to kill me in front of my fans, apparently to get 'famous'.

I have to use my mind, which has developed a lot by writing crime fiction, to get out of his range, that too alive.

Join me on this life-changing adventure of mine...

A Sneak Peak into my upcoming book -

Guilt Unfolds: The Ghoul Of His Past

Sequel to - 'Guilty Or Not...? : Secrets Of A Wanted Criminal'

Prolouge

His new victim's ear-piercing screams only made his smirk wider as his hands which were covered with a bloodthirsty, rotting ghoul's tatoo pressed the button once again.

The screams intensified as an electric current surged through yet another innocent's body.

"Partner...?" A hesitant voice met the ruthless creature's ears, "Forgive me for asking but...Are you sure they will come...?"

The hooded being growled in his guttural and husky voice while playing with his gun, "Mark my words...They. Will. Come."

He punched the already unconscious innocent man with his last words to emphasize his point.

The self-absorbed man didn't catch the tone of finality and anger in his partner's voice.

"But-" Before the arrogant man could argue any further his partner or Boss when it came to actual authority, rasped menacingly with a tinge of anger, "He was like my brother, I know him...She was the officer who managed to put *me*, behind bars...I know her...He will come...And so will she..."

His experienced fingers pulled the trigger without any hesitation as the innocent man's body went limp and fell to the ground, "I will have my revenge..."

His soon-to-be-dead partner made the foolish and last decision to open his mouth, "This is childish! We can just go there and kill them! In case you forgot, here, we both are partners and I get a say in things as well-"

Another gunshot silenced the voice criticizing him which made all the other men surrounding him shiver with fright yet the hooded man didn't even bat an eye before taking two lives within a minute. Nor did a single one of the men dared to oppose him. For them, his actions were law, only to be acknowledged and accepted, never to be questioned.

"I will have my revenge..." He muttered menacingly again as he lowered the gun that had taken thousands of lives.

He washed his blood-soaked hands as if rinsing the mud off after removing unwanted weeds.

He growled, "Clear the body"

"Yes, Captain," His men followed his command without any protests.

He smiled. He was going to have his revenge. Nothing in this world could stop him or so he thought. After all, he was the king of the illegal world. The one true overlord of the underworld. Who could possibly stop him?

It was a dark starry night. Storm clouds as big as mountains soon could be seen covering the entire sky like a veil. A thunderstorm was about to come and it wasn't related to the weather. The thunderstorm was flying inside an airplane high above the clouds like a hunting eagle.

The white airplane covered with blood-red stripes emerged, cutting its way through the dark clouds, and landed smoothly on the runway.

Out came the queen of thunderstorms, the ex-CIA officer, Hannah Gorgin, and ex-pseudo-assassin Soovin Cooper, along with their innocent, fifteen-year-old daughter Anna.

Anna ran towards the car waiting for them in excitement. The duo smiled at her and then, shared a grim look. Their eyes communicated even though their lips didn't move a single bit.

For Anna, it was a refreshing vacation to her Grandma's but for them, it was going to be something drastically different, a quest to protect the drastically different life they had created, a desperate attempt to keep the veil separating them from their dark and rocky past in place.

Hannah was well aware that in the process, her fingers wouldn't hesitate to send a certain someone to the depths of hell while Soovin had made up his mind to make that very person shake hands with the Grim Reaper at any cost.

"GG," Soovin muttered under his breath, his words filled with loath and a hint of disgust. The familiar name that used to fill his heart with warmth and a sense of brotherhood now made his blood boil.

"Gruesome Ghoul," Hannah gritted out the menacing name with even more anger and distaste as if she were spitting out poison.

"Here we come," The couple said together with flames of determination and anger behind their eyes.

When the woman who used to be the lioness of the CIA and is now the highest-paid detective and the assassin who made even the best officers go pale at the mere mention of his name are an emotionally bounded team, neither God nor Lucifer can save the one they are after.

The hands that wrote the note bringing the duo here might get more than what they bargained for when the CIA which is after the duo as well as the man is thrown into the mix as well.

Hell is about to break loose. Who knows how many lives will be caught in this tsunami when all of them cross paths?

Let the games begin...

Chapter 1: The Unanounced Arrival

"Han, will we ever be able to leave our past behind?" Soovin took me back with his question while he continued staring at the sun which was half hidden beneath the waves and ripples of the beach visible from the balcony.

I diverted my attention from the beautiful final light rays of the sun to him. No matter how hard he tried to hide it, I could see the anxiety and weariness in his emerald-green eyes. He absent-mindedly ran his long and thin fingers through his black, silky-smooth hair, the way he always did when he was feeling anxious. The sun rays kissed his angular jaw and reflected off his fair complexion. He licked his lips which were as red as a pomegranate.

"I...don't know, Soovin," My words seemed louder than they were when they broke the peaceful silence that was filling my heart with warmth. Prior to this, the only sound was Anna's soft and light snores.

"But," I continued, "What I do know is that we will find a way out of this and keep Anna safe...Together"

He finally moved his gaze towards me and smiled softly. I returned the smile as we both turned to look at Anna, sleeping peacefully in a white bed, barely visible over the blankets, and completely unaware of the dangers looming around. None of us had the heart to narrate our past and scare her with the solemnity of the situation. The way any breath could be our last.

She didn't need to know. She didn't need to worry. We wouldn't let him get near her.

I put my head on Soovin's shoulder as he stroked my hair absentmindedly. We were both lost in our own thoughts.

Mine revolved around the day we got the package and the note that had left me so shaken and petrified. Now, that was something new. The note was imprinted on my mind and I could still feel the blood stains it was bedecked with, in my pocket. The mere thought of it filled my heart with anger and the desperation to protect Anna at all costs. GG. Gruesome Ghoul. That was the name on the note. I was determined to find that man and send him straight to Satan in a state that would make Lucifer himself shed tears.

He had called Soovin his 'back-stabbing brother'. My heartbeat still fastened on remembering the terror-strick look laced with anger and pain on Soovin's face on reading it. I could only speculate about the relation between Soovin and him for we hadn't talked about the details of the note.

We realized that staying at our home wasn't the best option since the man already knew our address. He could harm Anna when neither of us was near her. Safety was our most critical concern. So, after talking about only our, or rather Anna's safety till midnight, we made the decision to pay my brother, Frank Gorgin, a visit.

I had used the spare key to get into the house when I remembered that Frank was probably still on duty. I of all people, knew very well how long CIA Officers had to work.

Frank was now in the CIA because of me (long story). So, we decided to tell him about the note. Although I will confess, that he is neither exceptionally bright nor very experienced, we decided that having more views on such a solemn topic was a must. After all, his pea-sized brain surely would have developed a bit after working in the CIA for three years.

The sound of a door opening broke my train of thought and pushed the budding flashbacks to the back of my mind. Soovin's grip on me tightened instinctively. After all, I wasn't the only one the note and package had managed to put on an edge.

I whispered so as to not wake Anna up, "Frank might be here"

Soovin nodded and both of us crept outside. We turned the corner only to meet the barrel of a familiar gun pointed directly at us.

My CIA reflexes still hadn't gone and I was about to twist the person's neck in self-defense. Judging by Soovin's tensed muscles, he was about to do the same. However, I stopped my attack mid-air on seeing Frank who lowered the gun as soon as he saw us.

I sighed in relief. My mind was prepared for the worst-case scenario that thankfully didn't happen.

I could see myself in his ocean-blue eyes. His eyes, bright rectangular face, and even his blond hair were exactly like mine. Given the similarities in our facial features, we could almost be considered twins. His narrow eyes widened and his pale lips lifted in a smile upon seeing us.

"Woah! What the heck are you both doing here?!" He exclaimed and gave Soovin a man hug who returned the favor with a grin.

I realized it was the first time he had smiled after the note and package had turned our life upside down.

"Well, surprise!" I said as a genuine smile appeared on my lips as well.

"Hannah Gorgin, you sneaky little cat!" He hugged me cheerfully, nearly crushing my ribs to pieces.

"Is Anna here too?" He asked while looking around, his eyes desperately searching for a lithe and small silhouette of a particular girl.

"She is sleeping in the guest room. We...kind of had to come urgently and...you know she can't sleep in the airplane," Soovin replied with a nervous and anxious edge to his voice.

Frank raised his eyebrows. Our grim faces said the rest as the humorous environment vanished into thin air and was replaced by a serious and tense atmosphere. The sound of insects in the garden just behind the sliding glass door was the only sound.

"What happened? Is everything good?"

I and Soovin shared a look. He nodded firmly at me, gesturing for me to do the honors.

"Well...Along with a...package, we found this at our doorstep," I reached for the note in my pocket.

The mere feeling of my fingers around it made my skin crawl as I recalled its contents. I took it out with shaky hands. It's neatly folded silhouette fitted right in the palm of my hand.

"You might want to sit, man," Soovin told Frank with a straight face.

Frank rolled his eyes at him muttering, "I am not a kid, buddy..."

However, the moment my clenched fist opened, Frank's eyes went wide upon seeing the bloodstains that bedecked the note and his legs backed up near the couch as his knees automatically bent, making him sit.

Despite the circumstances, I could feel Soovin smile faintly behind me. My short-lived smile disappeared as soon as it came, due to flashbacks threatening to cloud my thoughts. I brought the note on my palm closer to Frank for him to take it.

Still dazed and shocked, Frank gulped. Slowly and cautiously, he picked up the note, and started unfolding it...

My back-stabbing brother and the officer who put
me behind bars together, that too with a little
daughter. How sweet is that?

Wouldn't it be such a shame if something were to
happen to this cute, little, happy family?

I give you my warm greetings.

~ GG

(GruesomeGhoul, in case you forgot me, buddy)